SONGS

OF MY

LIFE

by Dory Robertson

Sophia
Eph 2: 10
we have become
His poetry
Dory

SONGS

OF MY

LIFE

Poetry and Prose
The Poema of God

Meet the Author
An Ordained Minister of
Pastoral Counseling, Ocala, Fl
One Foundation Ministries.

I've opened my eyes and taken my first breath. I reached out my hand and took hold of this new world, and I began to build my house on solid rock; my Foundation Stone. His Name is Jesus. Over the past 45 years with my Lord Jesus, He has spoken to me in poetry and prose to comfort and to give me the joy of His presence. Perhaps one of these will speak to you also.

Oh yes! He gave me hope and peace and every time He spoke to me, He revealed His song of songs; the music of His heart that brought me into heavenly places. His love lifted me out of the miry clay I had only known as my existence. His love has washed over me until now I can look in a mirror and see a woman who is worthy to be loved. Now like Mary, I sit at His feet, drinking in the majesty of His presence as He continues to sing His love songs to my soul and spirit. He gave His life for me and so I give my life to Him.

❤

We are His 'workmanship'
created in Christ Jesus
We are His Poema - His poetry.

In this book 'Poetry and Prose' He not only expresses how
He feels about His chosen ones, but also gives me
opportunity to express how much I love Him.

We love Him
because He loved us first
[1 Jn 4.19]

The Cover Painting Is by
the Author, Dory Robertson
Ocala, Florida
Songs of My Life
Second Edition 2018

I will put new songs in thy mouth
And thou shalt rejoice in the Lord thy God,
For He is a mighty God
He delivers and no man can bind
He lifts up and no man can pull down
Yea, He does valiantly,
and who can prevent Him?
[Psalm 40.3]

Take me and use me just as I am
Take me and use me Lord where You can
Filled with Thy Spirit,
Endowed by Your grace
I'll walk in Your love
Till we meet face to face.

In Christ I Will Always Be.
What joy is this has filled my soul
To be complete in Christ
Until that day and forever more
He is my heart – my life.

❤

Life is like a waterfall
It thunders deep in our soul
As it rambles on toward the sea
It conquers all in all
The rocks and debris are carried along
For a space and then let go
It settles down to be forgotten
As the river continues to flow
So all the sorrows of time gone by
Can be taken into God's arms
Carried along by His sweet love
That they shall no longer harm
So the waters of life flows over me
And the love of God prevails
They were hammered into
His hands and feet
By those old rusty nails
To conquer every sin and shame
In the glory of His name.

♫   As I come into your presence
efore your holy throne
I offer the sacrifice of love -
And to you I sing your praises
To worship you my Lord   ♫
May my life be always lived before you
In the shelter of your wings
In the secret place on high
And covered
By the Fatherhood of God . ♫

God created each of us
To fulfill His every dream
We each received a gifting
For more than we have seen
He's releasing His promise
We have waited so long
For His breath to enter our spirit
To impart His life and His song
He sings to our spirit
Our soul and our heart
For the joy that brings a dance
If you've never let yourself go
Why not give it a chance
The life of God within you
Will complete His creation
And there will never be
A chance of separation
For He created each of us
To fulfill His every dream
And heart has never known
Nor lips have ever said
Those things we've never seen
But He has promised!

❤

Some things were never meant to be
We make mistakes in the course of our life
We sometimes pursue a forbidden path
Not knowing the trouble out-of-sight
We try and try to make it work
Blinded by self-satisfaction
We ride along on stress and fear
And never take any action
We live a life of loneliness
As though it will be alright
But in the final course of life
It dissolves into the night.
So Lord Jesus, I give to You
The life You have given me
For the plans and purpose
You already have
Cause that's what was meant to be.

How Do I Love Thee Lord,
Let Me Count the Ways,
So Many in the Book You Wrote -
That Says
I Love You Because You First Loved Me
I Love You Because You Hung on That Tree
I Love You for the Mercy And Grace You Extended
For the Broken Heart Which Your Love Mended
Thank You Lord That You Died in My Place
Your Righteousness
Now Lets Us Meet Face to Face
How Do I Love Thee Lord, Now Let Me See
I Love Thee Because You First Loved Me.

Who are You God?
Do I know You - Can I know You?
You created me from the dust of the earth
Yet, You have given me everlasting worth
So Lord, who am I - Do You know me?
Can You see me -
Do You know where I am?
If I am the pride of Your life
If I am the prize You adore
Then can I know You? Can I see You?
If I am the one You desire
Then God, set my heart on fire
To pursue You - to find You
To enclose You in my heart
As I am in You
For I will never be satisfied
Until I know.

Lord, I sing a new song
There's a new song in my heart
I thank You for the music
You so gladly impart
You are the new song
The new song in my heart
So now I sing a new song
A new song to my Lord
For You are my song
You are my delight
You are the music in my heart
You are my song
You are my light
You are the new song in my heart.

Ever since I learned that You love me
Ever since You called me Your own
I don't want to see at a distance
I want to come right up to Your throne
Because You held back nothing
Even the life of Your Son
I want to hold back nothing
And so I give You my all in all
You said, "Come boldly before Me"
You said, "I've made the way"
You chose me, so I'm choosing
Lord, Call me to Your throne today.

Our Father God has created within Himself
A place called home
It is an ever expanding place
Of acceptance, warmth and love.
It was deliberately
Formed in the center of His Being,
Surrounded by His arms of love,
So that all His children would fit,
And be forever safe.

If a man love me,
he will keep my words,
and my Father will love him,
and we will come unto him
and make our home with him.
John 14.23

To know You Lord
is the hunger of my heart
To worship You in all I do
To feel Your love flowing through me
Like a river of the water of life
Coming from the throne of God
And from the Lamb
To be that tree of righteousness
Planted by Your river
To drink of Your living stream
To be all that You made me to be
Is the hunger of my heart.
Come into My throne room, child
Sit with me and drink of My love
Let My hand of grace overcome
The troubles and trials of life.
In your weakness
I shall strengthen you
In your failures, come to Me
And in time you will surrender
All of life that you could be.

♫ I'm Standing Here Before You Lord,
To Enter in Your Holy Presence,
I Lift My Hands and Heart
To Worship You,
♫ For You Are Lord,
You Are Lord,
You Are Lord.

Call me to the place where You are
That I may see Your face where You are
In the secret place where You are
I just want to love You
I don't want a thing for myself
I ask only that I may stay by Your side
You've given me so much in the past
I just want to love you
In Your secret place,
The pavilion You have chosen
Take me there to soar on eagle's wings
To see Your holiness and glory
In Your presence - my heart sings
Cause I just want to love You,
And to be where you are.

Draw me near, Lord, draw me near
Draw me into You heart
Draw me into Your presence
That I may know You -
That I may love You
That I may see You face to face
Draw me near, draw me near.

Make sweet melody, sing many songs,
That you may be remembered.
Isaiah 23.16

I sing to You my Father
In worship, praise and love
I sing to You my Father
In glory realms above
Redeemer, Savior, Lover, Friend,
My life I gladly give
So precious are You Lord to me,
For You alone I live
And Spirit how I long to be
Caught up with You on high
To live in realms of glory
There forever to abide. ♫

♫ Cover me Lord with Your Fatherhood,
Cover me over with righteousness,
Heal me now in the depths of my soul,
♫ And cover me over with love. ♫

You're a fire shut up in my bones
In Your presence
I desire to make my home
Transform me by Your power
To be bold and strong in this hour
Fill me with Holy Ghost
resurrection power.

❤

You are an original,
I made you like you are
I set aside all others,
And made for you a start
The beginning of a perfect you,
So we could become one
I birthed you and re-birthed you,
So you would never be alone
Each and every one of you,
fills a place in my heart
And I will never leave you,
We'll never be apart
I made each one individual,
Never like another
But I brought you all together,
So you could be brothers
Your spirit, soul and body
Are different in time
And when I gather all of you together -
You will be mine
So remember I made you
exactly as you are
And you will share in My glory
For as long as I Am your God.

With my eyes I will see Your glory
With my ears I will hear Your voice
I will stand in Your presence
And my heart will rejoice.

He gives strength to overcome
Strength to bear
Strength to go through
Strength to share.

I want so to live in the presence of God
To be one with You always in one accord
With the joy of us sharing one life
To be an end of disharmony and strife
If only I knew God,
What You want of me.

In Christ I Will Always Be.
What joy is this has filled my soul
To be complete in Christ
Until that day and forever more
He is my heart – my life.

Heavenly Blessings Defined in the Word,
Given to Us in the Name of the Lord,
Poured out from Heaven, Given as Leaven,
To Grow and Produce a True Son of God.
(Matthew 13.33 The Kingdom of God)

I would seek Your face Lord,
Not Your hand to give
I would seek communion,
For in this do I live
I've had many an answer
For special needs of mine
But they compare as nothing,
If I can't be Thine
The closeness of Your Spirit,
Your touch upon my heart
The knowledge You have given me
That we will never part
Oh Lord my God, my Precious One
Your love has lifted me
Because You've given all of You
I give my all to Thee.

God said to me...
Has anyone ever told you,
You are beautiful
Everything about you is incredible
You should have seen Me smile
The day I made you
You are to Me - beautiful.

I am loved by the Lord of Glory
I am crowned with mercy and grace
In His wondrous love I am growing
Till I see Him face to face.

What love is this cannot be ignored
It penetrates my heart and soul
No question as to where it comes
But needs our all in all
It's only Him - the One Who died for me
His name is Jesus - only Jesus
Whose love can penetrate
The heart and soul - Oh how He loves.

In Your Presence Is Fulness of Joy,
In Your Presence Is Fulness of Joy
For the Lord Is My Keeper,
My Glory and My Strength
In Your Presence Is Fulness of Joy
For You are holy, O so holy
You are holy, O so holy
And Your holiness surrounds me
Like a mantle over me ♫
And I worship You
Lord I worship You
Cause You are holy
And now I know
In Your presence is fulness of joy,
In Your presence is fulness of joy,
As I come into Your holy place
And approach Your holy throne,
In Your presence is fulness of joy.

What glory, oh what glory
To finally see His face
After all these years –
The crowning of His grace

When I see You in Your glory
When I see You face to face
And I humbly bow before You
So captured by Your grace
Then my eyes will be opened
My heart enraptured by Your love
Will I ever be able to breathe again
There in Your presence
Now I humbly bow before you
So captured by Your grace
And unto You my Lord I sing
In audience with my King.

Let Your glory fill this place,
Let Your glory fill this place,
With my hands lifted high
And my heart in surrender
Let Your glory fill this place
You are holy, oh so holy
And I hide my face in wonder
To approach You, oh my Lord
For You are holy
You are holy, holy Lord
And I bow before Your Name
To exalt You above all else
For You are holy
So Let Your glory fill this place,
Let Your glory fill this place,
With my hands lifted high
And my heart in surrender
Let Your glory fill this place.

You've always been faithful to me
I've learned time after time
To trust in You Lord, to rest in You Lord
You've always been faithful to me
So I'll rest in Your love
To keep my heart true
And I'll always be faithful to You.

The mind of Christ, it is my law
I choose to make it mine
Because Jesus obeyed that law
The power to do so - I bind
To my heart, my soul forever in Christ
Eternity, for all time.

I try so hard to surrender
all I have, all I am
But fear can have a front seat
To decide if I can
I want to live Your life,
I want to walk Your way
But every time I try Lord,
my imagination takes sway
If I could learn to trust You,
If I only could feel safe
Then my heart would truly give to You
All of me - all of me in sweet release.

Speak clearly to me Lord
While I am praying
Speak clearly to me Lord
Tell me what You're saying
I hear Your Spirit calling
And my heart responds to You
Speak clearly to me Lord
And call me to your throne.

No law against the fruit of love
No law that says we can't
No law that binds our heart from it
So take it, it can be ours
It's ours if we search for it
It's ours if we dare
Its ours cause he says it is
No rhyme or reason to declare
Because...
His Blood was shed for our healing
The cross brings an end to all strife
Jesus took captivity captive
Bound in his love, set free by his truth
Brought into his grace and his life.

I have a Father, He knows my name
He calls me to His side, again and again
He sees me where I am,
And where I will go
His plans for me too wonderful,
He reveals so I will know
Eternity - for at His side,
I'll rule and reign with Him
Because by His precious Blood,
He redeemed me from my sin
So I'm free to worship
With all my heart and soul
And live with Him forever,
In the Kingdom of His love.

Jesus, we adore You,
You've drawn us to this place
We bow down before You,
Humbly on our face
All the earth shall worship
At the throne of our King
Of Your great and awesome power,
We shall sing.

The bread was given for healing
The wine for inner life
To bring about why Jesus died
That we might inherit Your goodness
To walk in Your promise
To live in Your promise
A membrance of what You did for me
The promise of sweet release
The promise of eternity
And knowing Your grace and peace.

You Sent down Your Love
in the Form of a Man
Two Arms That Reached Out,
Two Feet That Walked My Path,
A Heart That Was Broken
And Tears That Were Shed,
With the Love
That You Sent down to Man.

Broken bread and poured out wine
Is what made the Savior mine
You alone would draw me near
With Your sweet song of redemption
As I cast my cares upon You
Bring me into Your embrace
That my soul shall be renewed
By Your sweet song of grace
Broken bread and poured out wine
Take me and make me, Thy will be done
Break me oh Lord till we are one
Of one accord to walk in Your way
One heart and one mind in Jesus I pray

Often did I look for You
Before I knew You cared
I didn't know You always
watched and waited
I said I'd be a good girl,
If only I would dare
So many years passed by,
The emptiness never abated
I also didn't know
You had Your perfect time
I was on Your heart, I was on Your mind
But one day there was a suddenly,
You came to meet me where I was
And the Word became flesh in me
And Your Spirit came upon me
And Your love enraptured me
Just becuz.

Only You can satisfy
The hunger of my soul
Only You can reach
The depths of my being
Its only You that has loved me
Its only You to Whom I can turn
You've put a longing in my heart
To answer the call, to surrender all
So let Your love burn - let my heart burn
Until I am one with You.

Knowing God, the desire of my heart
To know as I am known
To be like Him as promised
All that He has shown
His Word - His Revelation
Is a sweet book to devour
Its taste is better than honey
To reveal His mighty power
The changing of my heart, my life
Is what its done for me
That I might live forever
In God's eternity.

There's a new song in my heart
Holy Spirit fragrance flows
With the joy of His redemption
As His life within me grows
So cause me to come to Thy river,
Oh Lord, Cause me to drink fully
Of Thy love and grace
Cause me to humble myself before You
To enter into Thy Holy Place.

What is God saying here,
That your heart cannot agree
Are you troubled by your past,
You're afraid God can see
God is omniscient, omnipresent,
Knows it all
There's nothing you can hide from Him
He sees you rise and fall
He saw you in your Mother's womb
He saw you being birthed
He really did create you
To walk upon His earth
He wants you for His very own,
Forever at His side
So give Him all your heart and soul,
Forever to abide

Down in my heart, deep down in my heart
Lies the treasure that makes me a part
In newness of life
I've conceived His love
Borne on the wings of a dove
My brokenness no longer bears
The way I once was
For in newness of life
I've conceived His love
Now I'm His - just becuz.

Spending time in the presence of God
Is all I long for now
To see my Savior in all His glory
In perfect union will I bow
Into the presence of Jesus
Into Your presence I come
Only to see You face to face
How I long for this place called home.

Lord, with My Empty Cup I Crawled to You
Across the Desert Barrenness
Uncertain in Asking
Any Small Drop of Refreshment
If I Had Only Known You Better,
I'd Have Come
Running
With a Bucket!
Author unknown

The gift of grace never earned,
Cannot buy it,
Only asked if you will try it
Once you do, it is fulfilling
Once you do, it answers prayer
Cause once you do, His love is waiting
And He will always be there.

You are my glory, You are my covering
You are the only one that I adore
You are my Master, You are my Lord
You are the one that I live for
A life complete in You is what I seek
The mystery of darkness
Hidden in Your light
The secret place of Your presence
Hidden from my sight
Your promises have made me
What I hope for today
To seek the only one I love
To show me the way.

You left Your glorious throne for me
And came to be a man
To seek and save this long lost one
To make me to be all I can
Oh my Lord, my God, my King
I only ask this one thing
Restore my soul, restore my soul
That I may bring an offering

To know You as my Father
As revealed in Your Word
And to know who I am in You
Cause You are my Lord
At last I would belong
That in Your grace and mercy
I would be strong
Not led by all the darkness
That snares in unbelief
But to walk by Your Spirit
For my soul in sweet release.

I sing to You my Father
In worship, praise and love
I sing to You my Father
In glory realms above
Redeemer, Savior, Lover, Friend,
My life I gladly give
So precious are You Lord to me,
For You alone I live
And Spirit how I long to be
Caught up with You on high
To live in realms of glory
There forever to abide.

❤

We are each and every one
A reflection of God's glory
Not a copy of another
A facsimile to ponder
A one time gift
A one time wonder
Faces made and character blend
For only God to apprehend.

I am led by the Spirit of God
I walk in places unknown
Obedient to the will of God
I go where I am shown
To release His love to a hurting world
Is what He calls me to do
And I'll be faithful to only know
It's in His Name, He does it all
And He makes all things new.

Oh the grace of God that shines
As beacon in my soul
Delivering from a valley dark and drear
For this one to contain His love within
Will learn to live in God and have no fear.

One day God gave me a word and I looked it up.
'Contraband': [Thesaurus] Deception, Trap, Delusion.
Guile, Trick, Cheat, Wiles, Snare, Defraud, Lay a Trap,
Bait the Hook......
This is what satan does to us,
But watch this! What does God say?

I enfold you in My arms
To dry your tears and heal your heart.
Forever you belong to Me -
We will never be apart
I am your home, I am your heart
So seek Me first in all your ways
We are One right from the start
When you reached out your hand
You will always belong to Me
You are My contraband!
I bluffed the devil to buy you back
I tricked him with his own wily ways
I crushed his head and broke his power
Of authority over you
I defrauded him and cheated him
Out of the prize he thought he had
I laid a trap - a snare -
And he took the bait
And understanding came too late
Now nothing can separate us
You are Mine - you'll always be
The power of love that enraptured you
Will keep you for eternity.

❤

It's freedom that You've given me
To seek a place called home
Freedom from my slave sick soul
To be Your very own
To walk in grace and mercy
To know You as my Lord
And walk in heavenly places
According to Your Word
To know who I am in You
So at last I would belong
That in Your grace and mercy
I would be strong
Not led by all the darkness
That snares in unbelief
But to walk by Your Spirit
For my soul in sweet release.

We are the city of God
Brought forth by His glorious word
Joined together by the Blood of Christ
Cause we have made Him Lord
Our love for one another
Is because we are brothers
And we'll never come to an end
For Jesus has come to touch our hearts
And says He is our friend
So we come together in unity
To worship and praise our King
That glorious One - That holy One
It is to Him we sing.

God lives in me, He lives in others
He has made us all - brothers
Our hearts are joined to reflect His glory
This is His forever story
His plans were made before any time
So we could be His light to shine
Forever in His heart to stay
Cause He has shown us His eternal way.

Thank You Lord, for Your Great Love
You've Brought Me to Your Rest,
I'm No Longer Second Hand,
You've Given Me Your Best ❤

He is my Song of Praise
My Lord of Lords
The unforgotten phrase
The Word of words
The Prince of Peace
The Mighty God
A Father is He
To my restored soul.

You are my desire, my life is in You
To be at home with You,
To know Your love in my lonely heart
Is the longing of my soul, My One and All
To be at home with You.

One day I asked God,
"Why are You called Holy?"
He said to me...
*I Am called Holy because I Am unique -
Set apart from all creation.
All of creation is useless and of no value
But for what I give it.
I Am high above all else.*

*You are called holy
Because you are set apart
From all creation.
You are a son of God
Set apart to be My bride
High above all other creation for eternity
Your value is established in Me.*

Shut in with God in a secret place
Being with Him face to face
Sharing your heart, your soul, your mind
With only Him you will abide
There in the darkness of the night
Where only He will be the light
These precious moments one on one
You'll never forget until you're done

The Blood of the Cross
Put an end to all strife
In Jesus and His resurrection
Is promised eternal life

The will of God is all I need
And to His call I will ever heed
His glory is what He shares with me
My faith is that He cares for me
His love sets me heart on fire
He will always be my one desire
God wrapped me in His love and grace
One day I'll see Him face to face
I've been stamped and sealed,
I belong to Him
Cause He has set me free from sin
With Glory He has covered me
In Christ I will always be
I am His true inheritance.

Here in Your presence
I rest in Your love
Here in Your presence
In Spirit I move
Only what You ask of me
Will I choose to do Your will
But for this very moment
I will be still.

❤

This was given to me one day as I was experiencing
regrets and having an emotional response.

Don't go back there honey
To that dark and dismal place
I've made a way for you
To walk in My grace
Every tear you shed
Was for guilt and shame
But I've taken over your life
You're not the same
The Blood I shed on the cross for you
Has banished your shame and guilt
Remember when at prayer one night
I told My Father - '*whatsoever You wilt*'.
I died so you could walk free of regret
So you don't have to go back there
Walk by My Spirit, die to your flesh
And never have any fear
So let Me dry your tears,
And stay with Me a while
I know how you are hurting,
You've been defiled
If you will trust Me, I'll show you how
You may become all you were created to Be -
And we can start right now!

When We Stop Defining Ourselves by Our Failures,
But Rather as One Whom Jesus Loves,
Then Our Hearts Begin to Open
To the Breathtaking Discovery
Of the Wonder of Jesus Christ Living in Us.
Author unknown

When I'm standing in Your presence
When I see You face to face
In the wonder of Your glory
That You've brought me to this place
In the mystery of darkness
I can see why
You hide Yourself in wonder
From prying eyes
Those who have no spirit
To want to really know You
It's only curiosity
That brings them, it's true
But You are so available
To those who want to know
Who want to worship You
In all Your glory
Whose hearts are for the truth
The ones You have anointed
With Your sweet Spirit of love
We'll always be one with You
Forever.

The Chosen Fast
To loose the bands of my wickedness
To undo the burdens of my heart
To free me from oppression
That every yoke be finally broken.
[Isaiah 58.5-7]

Little did I know Lord,
it was for me You died
Little did I know
I could ever be satisfied
Little did I know
I could see You face to face
Little did I know I could feel
Your warm embrace
I didn't know I was meant
To know Your love
And that my inheritance
Was heaven above -
But I do now!

I only want to know You Lord
I want to seek Your face
But this can only happen
In Your secret place
So call me Lord, I will respond
I will run after You
As the deer pants for the living water
I will run after You
Call to me, Lord
I long to hear Your voice
For in my heart I will ever rejoice
And my soul every time
will respond.

The mystery of darkness
Hidden in Your light
The secret place of Your presence
Hidden from my sight
But since I have made You
My Savior, Lord and King
You've given what I long for
I only ask one thing
Your promises have made me
What I hope for today
To seek the only one I love
To show me the way.

The Blood and the Water
Burst from His side
The Blood and the Water
My Jesus crucified
The Blood and the Water
That paid the price
The Blood and the Water
My Jesus sacrifice.
The Blood and the Water
My Jesus died
The Blood and the Water
Brought forth His bride
The Blood and the Water
The dowry was paid
And into the tomb my Jesus was laid.
But death could not hold Him
And grave had to flee
The Resurrection and the Life
Paid the ransom for me.

You are my glory
You are my covering
You are the only one that I adore
You are my Master
You are my Lord
You are the one that I live for.
So Let Your glory fill this place,
Let Your glory fill this place,
With my hands lifted high
And my heart in surrender
Let Your glory fill this place
You are holy, oh so holy
And I hide my face in wonder
To approach You, oh my Lord
For You are holy
You are holy, holy Lord
And I bow before Your Name
To exalt You above all else
For You are holy
So Let Your glory fill this place,
Let Your glory fill this place,
With my hands lifted high
And my heart in surrender
Let Your glory fill this place.

I give the broken pieces
Of my life, my heart, my soul
Cause there's been so much sorrow
That has taken its toll.
Because You have spoken
Such love to my heart
How can I deny You
My all in all.

Enter in, Ye King of Glory
I've opened the door To my heart
Oh, hallelujah,
My Lord of Hosts
The gates of my mind
Are open to Your truth
Your gracious mercy
Has fed my soul
And my spirit
Rejoices in Your beauty.

There's no condemnation
to those in Christ
He's set us free from sin
When He came He brought His Kingdom,
Now He invites us to come in.
There's treasures and blessings
We know nothing about
Mysteries, secrets, darkness and light
But He calls us to search them out
We live in Christ, He lives in us
Such joy we have never known
But revelation comes to us
From the seeds we have sown.

We are a body
Connected to each other
And we are indeed
The keeper of our brother
We stand, we fall, and rise again
Encouragement we need
If we're to make it through this life
God's love and grace indeed
Please understand
That I'm different from you
In color or race or face
We're different in our culture
We're different in our tastes
God made us every one
To test us in our hearts
Will you accept me as I am
Will you love me in spite of it all
Or even because of it all
Will you thank God for me
Will you pray for me
You know we'll spend eternity together
So here am I, a part of you
We are a body - The body of Christ.

Into the throne room of Jesus
Into Your presence I come
Mercy and grace surrounds me now
As before You I humbly bow.

❤

Like poetry in the timeline of existence
I hear it and I choose to obey
But what if...so many what ifs.
I get distracted, called to another chore
From one thing to another
My mind is constantly my enemy
But what if I grab hold of Your peace
And call You to live in the depths of my soul
With the promise to overcome
And live my life so that
You are a part of me -
What then?

Oh Lord, our banner, Oh Lord, our banner
We build an altar unto You
You have prevailed over all our enemies
Jehovah Nissi - You are our God.
So we exalt You and glorify Your name
We exalt You and lift You high
We've built an altar,
You have prevailed for us
Jehovah Nissi, You are our God.

My spirit sings within me
My soul desires thee
To know Your love
To capture Your grace
To live inside Your warm embrace
This gift of life You've given me
I will treasure as long as I live.

Notes taken from "The Song of Songs".

We are one with our King, United with Him
We have become the Shulamite, Lover of God.
We will run away together into Your
Cloud filled Chamber, Your Holy of Holies.
I no longer live The Adam life,
He sees me as the lovely one.
No longer a veil between us,
It has been torn apart by the hand of God.
I am embraced with love in Jesus on the cross.
I am so involved with the cross
Where it all began
For I have spiritual revelation of the cross.
He has separated me unto Himself.
I am Tirzah - He is delighted in me.
Thou art beautiful, oh my love as Tirzah,
Comely as Jerusalem.
Adam wanted more than you
But You Lord, You will always be enough For me,
Yet I still want more of You.
For You keep growing my capacity for You
I rest in Your love until that day
You bring the joys of love to me,
So quickly pulling me into Your heart
You heal the brokenness within my soul.
You are always there for me.
Holy Spirit poured out, my land has been cleansed
And I enjoy union with Christ.
He brought me into a new thing
Through the wounded side of Jesus
And access to His grace,
He loves to hear me speak to Him.
In the realm of His holiness,
I am separated unto God With the joy of love.
I don't need the crowd,
Only in Him do I live. [Con't]

Continued:

> We go from religion to religion -
> Church To church - seeking the one
> True God - Seeking what it means
> To know God - To find real love
> In the arms of our Savior.
> But He is here all the time -
> Drawing us into His heart.

Now born into the Kingdom Of God.
Oh, thank You Jesus
For shedding Your Blood for me
That I might be Your Bride.
Your Word has become my life
And I say YES - YES. I will be your Bride
I will always trust You. Oh, live in me,
My Lord, For I cherish Your life in me.
I am covered by His glory.
I gladly give myself To The One Who
Gladly gave Himself for me.
No, I will never have enough,
I want more of You
That You might have more of me.
You healed my heart of stone
And my soul melted at the touch of
Your mercy. You taught me to love,
And it is Your love within me
That allows me to love others.
You are my life and I am Your prisoner.
You have invaded the depths of my soul
And brought Your light into my darkness.
Without Your sweet love -
What would life be?
I pray for a channel of love to others.
The attributes of Jesus,
The fruit of the Spirit,
Are growing in me as I live for Him,
He will never let me go.

❤

I am His garden of delight
To grow the fruit
That draws me near to Him
His love has captured me
Enraptured me
The lover of my soul
My Shining Knight
My ravished heart undone
I am truly overcome.
Come walk with me
As you walked with Adam
In Your Paradise garden
Come taste of the fruits
Of Your life in me.
[Galatians 5.22-23]

I traverse the circle of the earth
I sail the seas of the world
I wander the deserts
And climb the mountains
And yet - where am I
Who am I?
Behold the image of God
Created by His loving hand
Born to carry His love abroad
To those lost in darkness and shame
Behold the image of God
Created with His loving hand
All I can say
And confess with my heart
Here am I Lord - Here am I.

Not a one time expedition
Not a one time walk the block
Not a visit to a distant place
Whether we are known or not.
It is a one time coming in
Cause then you're one of us
He'll never let go of you
You'll never be lost.

Oh Glory,
God Has Saved Me for His Own.
I Long to Be in His Presence.

Father God Is a Second Chance
To Have a Dad,
When Many of Us Were Ripped Off.

With my eyes I will see Your glory
With my ears I will hear Your voice
I will stand in Your presence
And my heart will rejoice.

❤

This little Child was born to bring
His light into the earth
To show us where we belong
And Who has given us His worth
The One Who brought His love and grace
To those lost in sin
And wonder of wonders
He's inviting us in
The Kingdom of His mercy - peace
Enclosed within His heart
Has brought to earth, into our world
The power to impart
Our Redemption.

At the Cross, at the Cross
When I first saw the light
My soul was cleansed
My eyes were bright
I knelt down to worship
I knelt down to praise
I was drawn to Him
I was drawn to Him
My heart was filled
with everlasting love
And brought by His angels
To realms above.

Good morning Lord,
it's great to see the sun again
Good morning Lord,
I breathe the fragrance of a rose
And I remember
That my days are like a flower
And I'll be gone within the hour
That's why I say again -
Good Morning Lord.

Oh how He loves you and me
He died to save us,
Committed to life
Shed His Blood and His tears
Put an end to all strife
His grace and His mercy
Sets us free to love,
And the Father has called us
To His Kingdom above.

Into the throne room of Jesus
Into Your presence I come
Mercy and grace surrounds me now
As before You I humbly bow.

The will of God is all I need
And to His call I will ever heed
His glory is what He shares with me
My faith is that He cares for me
His love sets my heart on fire
He will always be my one desire
God wrapped me in His love and grace
One day I'll see Him face to face
I've been stamped and sealed,
I belong to Him
Cause He has set me free from sin
With Glory He has covered me
In Christ I will always be
His true inheritance.

Let Your glory fill this temple
Let Your Spirit fill me now
As I come before Your throne of grace
And as I humbly bow
You invite me to run
Into Your arms of love
To know that I'm forever safe
Your grace and mercy will cover me
And I am welcome in this place.
I have tasted and I have seen
That my Lord is forever good
And He is forever faithful to His Word
My Eternal One.

Tidbits or Pages...
I'm learning to live by the pages of God
To walk in trust and faith
To go each day to the Word and prayer
And surrender to His love and grace
No tidbits will do - I need it all
Cause I'm called to radical love
A tenacious life in Christ it is
In Him I live and move
To give all that I am and all I can be
To walk in His glorious way
The desire of my life,
The desire of my heart
I surrender all that is me
I'm learning to live by the power of God
To walk in trust and faith
To go each day to the Word and prayer
And surrender to His love and grace.

My spirit sings within me
My soul desires thee
To know Your love
To capture Your grace
To live inside Your warm embrace
This gift of life You've given me
I will treasure as long as I live.

❤

There's a Perfect Being within me
It's my born again spirit, a new creation
The anchor of my soul
Has been tossed within the veil,
His proclamation!
Forever faithful to keep me from falling
Forever loving me beyond my calling
He's the one to whom I bow
A future forever - and always now!
[Hebrews 6. 19-20]

We are the poetry of a God made Man
Completely by grace
And in faith do we stand
Stanza by stanza we grow to maturity
Always in Him do we stand, of a surety
Knowing what will become of us
When time has come to end
Cause we're trusting in a God
Who has made us His friend.

Oh Lord, the Reality of Your Kingdom
Has Totally Overwhelmed Me.
I Am Your Bride. You Have Chosen Me -
An 'Are-Not' of the World
To Manifest Your Glory,
To Be a Witness of Your Love
To Other 'Are-Nots'.
[1 Cor 1.27-28]

We are the Master's masterpiece
Formed by His own right hand
His image down to the last concern
To have at His command
He only wants to love us
And bring us freely alive
But in our rebellion and pride of life
We've turned to our own archive
We were created to be His own
To live in His tender care
So He did what was of the gravest sort
To die - shed His Blood - lay bare
On the cross of indignity
He hung before His nation
He carried out His Father's wish
To reconcile creation
So now we are His masterpiece
Reborn for Him alone
To walk the path He plied for us
Until we get back home.

We're the mighty sons of Israel
We are strong in the Lord
We're the mighty sons of Israel
Cause we feed on the Word
Let us arise and go forth in our God
We will conquer every foe
Our inheritance is our redemption
And in His name we will go.

The Father breathed on Adam
He became a living soul.
Jesus breathed on His disciples
They were born again - A living spirit.
But He didn't stop there
He breathed on us all.
John 17.20-24

Out of the dust of yesterday
Comes the foundation of my life
Established in the heart of the Spirit
An edifice of praise
A house of worship
To celebrate our King.
He's the origin of our beauty
The Master of Kingdom rule
To gather the pieces of straying emotions
That was scattered by devious strife.
He pulled me out of dread darkness
To enter His Kingdom of light
So I celebrate my King of kings
And continue to walk in His sight
Grace, grace, oh glorious grace
I am now complete in Him
To live His life in love and peace
And know I'll always be safe.

*For God is working in you, giving you
the desire to obey him, and the power
to do what pleases him.*

The Mighty God of Creation has drawn up his plans.
He has chosen to build his dwelling place within his
people. The architecture must be perfect with no spot
or wrinkle; cleansed unto holiness; sound unto
righteousness; yet no hammering will be heard in this
temple. *Neither hammer nor axe nor any tool of iron
heard in the house, while it is in building.* Each brick
will be laid with tears of repentance. Each column is
held fast on the humble knees of prayer. The ceiling
will be constructed of praise and worship; the
foundation is built upon no less than The Rock, Our
Redeemer, Our Glorious Lord and King,
JESUS MESSIAH - Our Chief Cornerstone.

*For God is working in you, giving you the desire to
obey Him and the power to do what pleases Him. We
have a building of God, a house not made with hands,
eternal in the heavens ... desiring to be clothed upon
with our house which is from heaven, so that, being
clothed, we shall not be found naked, and built upon
the foundation of the apostles and prophets, Jesus
Christ himself being the chief corner stone, in whom
all the building fitly framed together grows into a
holy temple in the Lord; in whom you also are built
together for a habitation of God through the Spirit.*

Be Still And Know That I Am God.
Do You Really Believe
That What You Believe
Is Really Real?

We are made in the image of God
Special to Him alone
He waits so patiently for us to be ready
For the trumpet to call us home.
He's prepared such a special place
That we may abide in Him
Forever to bow at His feet in praise
And walk in His love and grace.

Come and sit by My side
Come and sit by My side
For you are my lovely bride
You have caused Me to heal your land.

Your revelation so sweet to my ears
Will speak of Your love
Down through the years
Growing and knowing this life in You
Such a joy to my heart
Is knowing the truth
You really are the only way
And I want to walk in Your path
So show me each step that I must take
To know You is all that I ask.

At the time of the evening sacrifice
I offer You all I possess
At the time of the evening sacrifice
At my altar, my heart says yes
There's a purging fire
Revealed in Your Word
I seek to cleanse my soul
That Your throne alone be exalted
I receive You as my all
So I come to You at the time
Of the evening sacrifice
And I long to abide in Your presence
Forever more.

The Kingdom of God
has come in its power
Alive and well in this very hour
By the Sword and His Spirit
We live by the Word
Because, sons of God
We have made Jesus Lord.
Forever we will conquer
The enemy of our land
Cause the Kingdom of God
Has come
AND...

One day during worship at Church, the Lord gave me a vision. I saw what seemed to be a wall that had an alcove and within the alcove was a stunning green gem, an emerald that shined with brilliant light so dazzling, it took my breath away. I asked the Lord where is this wall that held such a jewel? As He stood before me, there opened in the center of His Being, the alcove containing this brilliant light and green emerald.
He said to me-
This is my Bride, I carry her
within me wherever I go.

Green Is the Color of Life,
and the Bride derives Her Life
From Our Glorious Savior,
Lord and Bridegroom, Jesus Christ.

The end here, is just the beginning
Going on with God
A future worth its waiting for
To carry His staff and rod
To walk in His authority
With grace, and mercy and love
And be with Him forever
In His home above.

❤

Listen for the sound of My coming
No horse or trumpet blare
Only the sweet whisper in your heart
Will let you know I care
I hear the voice of your return
To seek Me, you always search
For what I have to offer you
As love within you burns.
I've loved you 'ere since time began
I'll love you to the end
Cause I know you always look to Me
And I'll always be your friend.

Here I am again Lord,
Looking for You
To show me how to live
To show me how to love
You have become my dearest friend
So walk with me until the end.

All the women who formed the nation of Israel
were barren,
But then they had a child of promise.
And with all these children,
God removed
The reproach of His people.
And then came Jesus.

WHAT WOULD HAPPEN
IF WE REALLY FOLLOWED JESUS?

I am planted by the Tree of Life
And I walk in the Kingdom of God
Never ashamed, never condemned
I walk with His staff and rod
No fear will ever live in me
I am strengthened by His grace
His wrap around power was given to me
When I began to walk by faith
Fruitful - yes I am in Him
And always attached to the vine
Cause He's wrapped around me
And I'm wrapped around Him
And He will always be mine.

By the fragrance of Christ, His Church
Should be a wonderful blend of
spices and flavors so as to attract
Even the hardest of hearts.
The world has a counterfeit aroma,
'You can have what you want
When you want it. Just follow me'.
Having what we want brings satisfaction,
But only for the moment....
He was pierced and crushed,
A sweet savor to the Father.
But He took on our filth
And we became
A sweet fragrance of His holiness.
[Isaiah 53; 2 Corinthians 2.15].

Abundant mercy
Grace to the fore
Came with the Christ
That much and more
He brought His Kingdom
He brought the gift of life
And through His death
Came the end of strife
The law was dead
It is finished came the declaration
For in the beginning
Came the preparation
He knew all along what was destiny
Yet He came to propose
To bring a war, to bring an end
The enemy at last
Was revealed and disposed.

It's a Good Thing to Be Kept in a Place
Where We Have to Fight for Our Life,
If it Means Drawing upon God
For Spiritual Power.
[T. Austin -Sparks.]

The enemy builds a counterfeit city
God is rebuilding the original.
His city, the legitimate - and we know
What the finishing touches will be.
Let's focus now on the journey.

The Lover of my soul,
I give Him my all
To remember He's the One
He died for me upon a tree
He did it all, it's done!
Am I dating Jesus - or married to Him
Trusting Him as He commands
He knows my heart and I know His
I find safety in His hands.
He leads me by still waters
And calms my weary heart
I'll always love my Savior
Yes, I'm married to Him
We'll never be apart.

I am a friend of God
I am...I am
I walk with Him
Every time I can
He sings to me
His songs of love
And takes me to His realm above
We walk together hand in hand
My name is Enoch
Come join us if you can.
Genesis 6.23-24

❤

Yu are writing a gospel
A chapter each day
By deeds that you do
By words that you say
Men read what you write
Whether faithless or true
Say, what is the gospel,
According to you?
[John R. Rice]

Psalm 23
The Lord is my Shepherd
I shall not want
I need not have any wants of my own.
I can walk in His good pleasure.
He is making me suitable
For His habitation.
He leads me to a place of rest.
He wants to bring me back to what
He intended for me in the beginning,
From which I strayed so far.
He's putting me back together
The way I belong, pleasing in His sight,
To fulfill His purposes for me.
I will go forth and rise above
In exaltation, over the evil before me.

The Knots Prayer

Dear God,
Please untie the knots
that are in my mind
my heart and my life.
Remove the have nots,
the can nots and the do nots
that I have in my mind.

Erase the will nots, may nots
and might nots that may find
a home in my heart.
Release me from the could nots
would nots and should nots
that obstruct my life.

And most of all, Dear God,
I ask that you remove from my mind
my heart and my life, all the 'am nots'
that I have allowed to hold me back,
especially the thought
that I am not good enough.. Amen.
[signed, Author Known to God]

Where Are You?
And What Footprints
Will You Leave Behind?

❤

Daystar of the morning
Dawn before our eyes
Rise that we may see Your face
Prince of Paradise
Clothe Yourself in splendor
Clothe Yourself in might
Trail of supernal righteousness
Quintessence of all light.
[Song of the Bride - Anna Roundtree]

Old king Saul was a major of all
In the college of disrepair
He knew not one but many ways
To discredit, destroy
Those under him.
For jealousy, anger and lack of faith
Another Korah was born.
[Numbers 16]

Hello again
I'm here to say
I'm so glad to be alive
You've captured my soul
You've given Your all
How do I say thank You
Cause I'm so glad to be alive.

Through faith and patience Is love born
Derived from the Father's heart -
It all began from eternity,
That was the start. He told me,

I did this because I knew How much
you would need My Love, Trust that I
will never leave - now you're
part of My family.

So many times I've fled to you
With anguish in my soul
So many times I've bowed my knee
And gave my all in all
I didn't know there was so much more
To test my heart of faith
But I am learning Lord
That You've got my back
And You'll always keep me safe.

Are we seeing the Kingdom of God
By the beam of a flashlight
Or is the overhead light turned on.

❤

Some time ago I was in a Church service
praising and worshiping God.
There was in a vision before me,
a meadow of beautiful lilies.
God said to me,

*"When My People Put on
The Garment of Praise,
They Are Clothed More Majestically
than King Solomon".*

The Temple priest was the only one allowed to burn
the incense. As its essence rose before the Lord,
carrying the prayers of Israel, so now we may freely
come. The gift of His priesthood is ours,
as our Great King/Priest Jesus,
the Lion of Judah, stands before the Throne
calling us into the Holy of Holies.
He opened the door,
INTO THE PRESENCE OF THE FATHER.

*Let my prayer be set forth
before thee as incense;
and the lifting up of my hands,
as the evening sacrifice.*
Psalm 141.2

Stuff in the past will stay there
Cause Jesus packed it all up
And carried it all to Calvary
And into the depths of hell
When He arose victoriously
He gave me the crown of life
And said to me, no more weeping child
For you, now, all is well.

Here I am for You Lord
Here I stand for you
Mighty Man of war
You give Your people power
To contend with the enemy of their soul
Grace and mercy in this hour
You enable truth to overcome
To prevail for a heart full of grief
And all our yesterdays vanish
As we meet with a Heart
Full of love to release
Oh yes, here I am for you
And here I stand for you
Faithful in all my ways
Faithful for all my days
For my sweet sweet Spirit of God
Has surrounded me
And impounded me
Enraptured by His love
His arms mighty and strong
Determined to make me know I belong
Oh yes, here I am for you
And here I stand for you
Mighty God of love
Mighty Savior of my world.

The presence of God
Is His wrap-around love
He hovers over us
From His throne above
We are always in His sight
Every day and every night
So be still my heart and rest in Him
And know that His Spirit lives within.

As the earth holds its breath in awe of You
Your presence surrounds us now
How great, how great is our God
As before You we bow
Your love has captured the soul of man
We can do nothing more
But to worship the King of kings
To magnify Your name
To walk by Your Spirit
To love You in our deepest part
To join with You heart to heart
Because we have been restored.
I hear the rolls of thunder
I hear them shout His name
The King of Glory
The king of Glory
Over and over again
And for love He responds to us
As He touches each of our lives
To pour out in great abundance
His storehouse of awesome grace.

Bound together by love's strong cord
Never again to be lost
Cause the Master of all eternity
Has paid the price - what the cost
He left it all He gave His crown
His place in the heavenlies
He laid it down
He became just like me
To die on a tree
He gave it all
So I could be free.

I Am His Holy Place, He Lives in Me.
I Am the Temple of the Living God.
I Give You All Honor, Praise and Glory.
Shut in with God in that secret place
Longing to hear Your voice.
I have no other agenda
I am here by my free will choice.

How can I say, Lord
In my feelings or my works
That as a child of the Kingdom
I'm part of Your Church
To know You as You know me
To love as You love
To grow in grace
To be an Enoch
To walk in realms above
Cause You promised me.

All creation worships You
All creation moans
The Lamb of God, reality/truth
Has risen to His throne
To recall His people, to bring them in
His Blood shed - Him alone
No other could redeem us
He took Adam's place
For mercy, love, compassion
An abundance of His grace
To awaken a soul long dead in sin
To open a door to let us in
And bring us home to Him.

A double portion of pleasure and grace
As we see God face to face
Oh the glory, true rapturous love
Coming down to us from heaven above
I love You Lord Jesus
I'll love You to the end
I'll forever be faithful
Cause You made me Your friend.

What Is the Meaning of Life?
To Know That We Were Created to Know God,
And to Become Like Him
This would be enough to know
For this is the fulfillment of life.

Only found because He knew
It would be a lifelong search
To find my path, to find my hope
To find what I am worth.
I couldn't sense reality
I couldn't find my way
Until Love stepped in
And took my hand
He touched my heart
With His wrap-around presence
And brought me to His promised land.

Grace and mercy from the throne
He has called me to be His very own
Your name is written in my soul
Because You gave Your all
For redemption now is the gift of life
And gave me a chance to believe
You've broken the powers
That ruled the world
And Your promises I receive
So to our awesome Jehovah God
I give my heart, I bow my knee
And celebrate Your holiness
As I stand on Your Word
Grace and mercy will follow me.

There is none like You, God of heaven
Who sent His Son as Holy Leaven
To grow from a tribe
Of a wandering nation
A people who would blend as one
One body - one mind -
One life - one cause
To worship the God of creation
What a sensation to be brought
To Your throne
And know we belong to You alone.

Down through the corridors
Of timeless space
There stood a man with glory on His face
Awaiting the Word to go forth in power
He stood ready for the appointed hour
The timing was perfect to enter the race
To show them His Father - face to face
But before that was done
There was a tree
His destiny was carved in stone
Yes, His death must surely be
So He entered this drama alone
It would not, could not be changed
That was so long ago arranged
And there He hung before the world
So the plan of God could be unfurled
To show me the love of a God made man
And set me free to be who I am.

The Sea of Glass [Revelation 15.2].
Nothing hidden in the Nature of the Bride.
Transparency.
What will be seen ?
Righteousness or rebellion.

Free choice, He says, it's up to me
I can say and do what I want to be
But oh, the consequences of this freedom
Can only lead to darkness and death
Is there none that can save me
As I wander alone
Oh yes there is...the Breath of God
A lamp to my feet, a light to my path
His Glory and His Love to encompass me
His inheritance to astonish me
The joy of His presence makes me laugh
And His love covers me
At LAST.

I am the righteousness of God in Christ
Created by His own right hand
He saw me back in the beginning
Destined to take the land
To live in the glory of the Kingdom of God
Inheriting all that He is
Destiny, He planned it all
To sit at His own right hand.

Fallen, fallen into the abyss
To satan's joy and glee
He fully thought this was the end
Father would have no friend
But out from the grave
Victory came a surprise
To everyone who knew
He gained the ground
He won the war
He did it all for me and you.

As the earth holds its breath in awe of You
Your presence surrounds us now
How great, how great is our God
As before You we bow
Your love has captured the soul of man
We can do nothing more
But to worship the King of kings
To magnify Your name
To walk by Your Spirit
To love You in our deepest part
To join with You heart to heart
Because we have been restored.

❤

I was so pretentious at the start
In my heart
I thought I had to prove
That He loved me
But as time went by
Between me and Him
He grabbed me and pulled me in.
Now I see with clarity, reality
The Kingdom ruled by grace
No pretense, no compromise
I see Him face to face.

Not enough said Adam, I want to explore
Not what I have with You Lord,
I want much more
There's other ways and things to do
On the other side of the gate
To taste and see the wrong and right
And where should I put my faith
I'll try this, and I'll try that,
And then I will decide
But OH! If I could just turn back
I know now, I gave up my life.

In the early, beyond creation
Lived a God and King
And all the angels worshiped
Continued their hearts to sing
But He desired a people
For love and for peace
So He created them
And then released
The grace that reigned forever
Was a product of His love
Spread out before His people
From His Kingdom above.
But then there came one
Forever dissatisfied
And gathered a multitude
To them, he lied
Dishonor and grievances
Was his accusation
For this God and King
Who ruled their nation
Rebellion was the answer
To make him lord of all
And those who lived beneath his lies
Responded to his call
Such cunning and deception
Created his crown
For he would have his nature
Ring with renown
But this glorious God and King
Would not be cast aside
For He was loved and worshiped
Far and wide
His power, grace and mercy
Far outweighed   [Con't]

The usurper who thought he could win
A war with just one raid
He didn't know his plans were known
That he was far outnumbered
And those whose legience
To faith and truth
Were more than he could plunder
Thrown out of the Kingdom
To create his own
He thought he'd won at last
He was blinded by his arrogance
Cause victory would not be shown
Many who would bear their sin
He denied them will to live
He drove his victims to their death
For that's all he could give
But this King watched
With grace and love
For the perfect time to act
And when it came He stepped aside
From His glory - to renew His pact
He made a covenant at the start
For a people meant to be
He shed His Blood, He died for us,
That we would be free
Now this liar, deceiver, rebellious one
A dilemma findeth him
He has no crown
He has no throne
He lost it all to Ha Shem.

I am a new creation
Made by the hand of God
To rule and reign with Him
To carry His staff and rod
His eternal kingdom
Was made for you and me
To walk and talk in His garden
Like Adam and Enoch
His friend we will be
His grace and mercy
Has called us there
Oh glory, how He loves.

Another Lamb, This One Unique
Has Shed His Blood For You
On the cross He was impaled
So we would know the truth
He bore our shame, our guilt, our sin
For our soul set free
To make a place for Him to live
Within you and me.

Oh, could I tell,
ye surely would believe it
Oh, could I only say
What I have seen
How should I tell
Or how can you receive it
How, till He bringeth you
Where I have been.
Author unknown

There's the wonder of a butterfly
Two souls contained in one
Yet destined to separate
To join the beauty
Of a resurrected life.

Open my heart to Your glorious ways
I want to see You face to face
To be in Your presence
To walk hand in hand
Oh what glory is this pleasure - and -
To know Your love, Your Joy, Your peace
Will never be beyond my reach
It's there for me when I awake
To walk with You for another day.

Seek Me until you find Me
I'm here right now
Waiting till you turn your face
Your heart, your mind
To seek My grace
What do you need?
What do you need
To fulfill your dream
What do you need?
My answer will come
When you see that
All you need is Me.

Thank You Lord For loving me
For letting us hang You
On that tree
The Blood You shed
Broke every curse
But separated from You -
That was worse
So thank Your Lord
For the Blood You shed
It brought us back
Cause that's what You said
So long ago in Covenant
Your promise came to pass
You revealed the Father,
We're home at last.

I'm not my own, I belong to Jesus
Endued with power in this very hour
To vanquish the enemy that taunts me
In the memories that haunt me
As I try to sleep
But remembering my soul to keep
In the heart of the Very God
Who stole me away from
The vicious thief
Who thought he could conquer -
Overcome
The One Who shed His Blood
But didn't know this Very God
Was the One Who would conquer him.

Your love comes down
Like a fire in my soul
It draws me into Your presence
Your will be done against my will
To consume my all in all
And I surrender to Your holiness
To yield and be still
So speak to me, Father
Hold me close to Your heart
Your greatness unimagined
I want to be a part
Never would I walk alone
I need Your life and grace
To know You as You know me
Together - forever In Your embrace.

Capitulate, renovate
Over the hills the river runs
Just where it wills
I can't say what it will say to me
I only know I have to stay and see
For it leads me to the Master's heart

Thank You God that You hung on that tree
Thank You for the Blood
That was shed for me.

Created in His own image
There stood a man called Adam
He opened his eyes to the God of love
And raised his hand to adore
He saw the beauty of the earth
The life that wandered about
He gloried in his walks with God
The talks that taught Him secrets
The universe was made for him
He marveled at its span -
But that was just not enough
He wanted someone else
Companion, friend, lover, a mate
And put her at the first
Too vulnerable - she believed the lie
He watched her glory fade
So he lost it all to a lesser god
And inherited shame and disgrace.

Amazing grace, how can that be
To save a sin sick one such as me
You saved my soul
And gave the Spirit of life
I no longer live with the spirit of strife
You conquered my enemy
Gave me power to live
As the just will have faith
And the power to give
Overwhelming love How can that be
That You died in my place Ever to be free
Oh glorious One - Lover of my soul
Because You have given
I give You my all.

The bricks and the mortar
To build my house
Were formed by God's mighty hand
He used my tears to bind them together
My joy to stack them high
He uses peace to smooth the glue
His righteousness squares my soul
His love has laid the roof in place
And His grace has opened the door
No hammer is heard in building this house
Just the stillness of His voice
For He has prepared for fellowship
My home inside Himself.

In Gethsemane and Calvary
You gave all You had
To pay for someone else's sin
But God, I'm so glad
My sin was just as deadly
To send me far from You
But in mercy, grace, compassion
You paid the price
You died my death
For love of Your creation
You made us all brand new.
Thank You, Jesus.

The love of God is the poetry of heart
The wonder of all creation
To see the expanse of the universe
And wonder why He made us like Him -
Preparation!
His plan was hidden from prying eyes
So nothing would stay His hand
The course of His - Story
Would complete the round
He will have His holy nation
The Blood and Water washed us clean
From the stain of sin and shame
He died in our place, There is no blame
He has made us a son - redeemed.

Only the One who could save us
Only the One who would die
On the cross of shame and obscurity
He took sin for you and I
No one understood the why of it all
Even His friends protested
satan was glad to be rid of Him
He would not be contested
We know now He made it clear
It was all for sin to end
When it came down to seeing Him there
They thought they'd lost their friend
Their grief was just too much to bear
Until that Sunday morn
Because on Resurrection Day

A New Man Was Born

I hear the rolls of thunder
I hear them shout His name
The King of Glory - The king of Glory
Over and over again
And for love He responds to us
As He touches each of our lives
To pour out in great abundance
His storehouse of awesome grace.

We all wear a mask, its name is fear
It will show itself when people come near
It's covered my soul for a very long time
I welcomed it, harness and all
I knew it would keep me lest I fall.
I hide behind it, 'tis my friend
He'll stay with me until the end.
But God says no.. It has to go!
It's not your friend at all
Come with Me, I'll set you free
Please heed My call.
So I took the chance
And shed my mask
And all I did was ask.
Jesus did it all.

The Difference Between
Covenant and Contract
Is Relationship.

He was the mercy seat on the Ark of God
Where the Blood was sacrificed
He was the One the high priest met
Behind the veil where sin was judged
Abraham saw His face
Isaac took His place
Jacob met Him as a ladder
And Moses met Him in the fiery bush
Joshua met the Man of war
The Judges did preside
But little Samuel had to prophecy
The death of the priest Eli
Of all the kings who were enthroned
David stood the best
And on his seat will come the One
Who will finally give us rest.

If anyone boasts, let him only boast
In all the Lord has done
He has taken the downtrodden
And with Him, made them one
The puny, the powerless and shameful
He raises above the proud
The nobodies, He made somebodies
So we can shout aloud
To be foolish and feeble before the Lord
And humbly bow before Him
Our gracious God has opened the door
And bids us to come in
The wedding supper is all planned out
And welcomed are we who were lost
He found us and raptured
Our broken heart
And loves us - just because.

Here I am again Lord
Dancing to the melody and tune
Of Your mercy and grace
Awaiting that glorious day
When I will dance before Your face.

When I see my Savior
When I'm standing face to face
Then I'll know
I'm in the right place
The glory that belongs to Him
Will brighten every soul
Cause He came to give His life
For every nation of the world
And as the redeemed
Gathers round the throne
We will know we are safe
We will know we are home.

The excellence of this power
is of God, not of man.
And the glory that You have given Me,
I have given them,
that they may be one
just as We are one.
John 17.22

The Spirit of the Lord is upon me
To know the Word
And the gift of revelation
To have the wisdom just to know
Of His love for every nation
To set the captives free
To know as He knows
And walk in restoration
To have the freedom this very hour
That we need to live this life
With God within
Who gives the power.

The presence of God
Is His wrap-around love
He hovers over us
From His throne above
We are always in His sight
Every day and every night
So be still my heart and rest in Him
And know that His Spirit lives within.

We are not of this world
We belong in heavenly places
This is what God intended
So we could walk in His graces
A school to test our trust
Will we abandon God
If things get too rough
Or will we abandon our own agenda
And lean on God
His cause to surrender.

It doesn't matter who I was before
It matters who I am now
It doesn't matter what my life used to be
What am I making it now?

To know God -
To know beyond a shadow of a doubt
That He is Sovereign
And that my life is in His care,
This is the unshakable foundation
On which I stay my soul.

❤

My God, in the name of Jah
Strode on to the scene one day
He saw the pain - we were to blame
He knew we needed correction
First He laid down the law
Then He showed us the way
To walk in reality, truth
Then it all came to pass
When at last
He gave us the right direction
So how can we forget
The real name of God
They changed it to suit their need
He is not LORD - I am not 'he or she'
I have a name
So does He - the same as His Dad's
Yahshua of glorious fame.

We are covered by the Blood
And our sacrifice is pure
Holy and acceptable to God
Washed in the water of the Word
And to Thee my God and Savior
I give my all in all
And worship You forever
As my only Lord
So thank You for Your sacrifice
That makes mine all the best
And thank You for the blanket
That brings me to Your rest.

At the cross - at the cross
Where Jesus was crucified
The law of sin and death
Was at last satisfied
He took the thorns into His brow
To assuage the curse of earth
The nails in His hands and feet
Showed us what we're worth
Captured by His love for us
He hung upon that tree
Nothing could cause Him
To shun the shame
For His only desire
Was to cause us to know
The power of His Name
Yahshua.

What does it mean for me to know God
To have invested in me His living Word
To know that I've been loved
From the time of my birth
To know that I have everlasting worth
To have Him live inside of me
So I can be what I ought to be
What assignment has been laid out
That I can live in His blessings
The would bring about changes
To glorify Him as He arranges
That my life would be
Forever in His hand that He
Could bring me to His highest plane
That His Spirit would fill me
Again and again
With the love that brought me face to face
With the God that I can know.

As the sun rises in the heavens
So You have risen to greater glory
That the knowledge of the Lord
Would break every chain
To reveal Himself again and again
To those who wander deep in sin
To reveal His love again and again
That they would turn from evil ways
That they would gaze
Upon the glory and the light
Of the One Who died in their place
To make them right
In the eyes of our righteous God
Who alone took the power of sin
And broke it - took our shame within
He lived our life - He died our sin
And gave us His life, the new to begin
To abide with our God
And know He is love
For all eternity
In heaven above.

We are made in the image of God
Special to Him alone
He waits so patiently for us to be ready
For the trumpet to call us home.
He's prepared such a special place
That we may abide in Him
Forever to bow at His feet in praise
And walk in His love and grace.

No more sorrow and pain
Wash me Lord, once again
From the power of death and sin
Its back is broken, Its head is severed
And who shall reign
In the stead of darkness
But that King - the Lord of all glory
Seated on His throne of light
With grace and mercy poured out
To all the lovers of God
That we may walk
In the shadow of His wings
And raised from the dead
Eternity - to live our life in Him.

The door, the door
The door to the kingdom
How can I find it, How shall I know
Where is the one Who holds the key
Who is the One to open for me
The last word was uttered
Then came the last breath
He paid for it all, He gave in to death
But the door to the kingdom
Came alive to His voice
It was torn in the middle
He opened the way
Through sacrifice that day
So we can rejoice
And respond to His call
To give our all
To the One who holds the key
To the only door that sets us free.

Of all the people
That ever walked the earth
He made us different
And counted our worth
He saw deep within our soul
The hunger for fulfillment, to have it all
But soon we had to learn the cost
For we were among the lost
How can there be an escape from this path
How can there be true life at last
We had to look to another way
Outside our selfish heart, to pray
There would be a Savior,
Redeemer somewhere
That could see our grieving soul From there
To come and rescue our sin-sick heart
To touch our life, and make us live
For He had everything to give
That He would die for us
And we would die for Him.

And all the angels worshiped Him
And wondered on that day
That He would send His Spirit
To the womb of a young girl
To show us His truth
To show us His way
To bring to the world
The meaning of love and mercy
Oh Captivator - capture me
In Your web of reality
So all the lies that I've believed
Are broken down and buried
In the Sea of Tranquility.

There paraded before the mass
Stood the Holy Man of God
Ready to do His Father's will
To set us free at last
Planned before hand in heaven's realm
For when the time was right
He brought His kingdom with Him
His glory and His light
The kingdom is within you
He said - A promise to all
If only you would listen
And heed My call
It is salvation to you who would come
I've prepared a mansion
A place called home.

Born to die
This man of glowing grace
He came to show the Father
To a fallen race
With forgiveness in His heart
And love in His hands
He determined to walk
The breadth of His land
So many people dying in sin
He opened His kingdom
For us to come in
But first came the cross
In our stead He died
For sin had imprisoned
His people through lies
The only solution
To set us free
Was to take our place
Born to die for you and me.

Yes - yes Jesus
I will look for You
Through time and space
Until I know You -
Until I see You in all Your glory
For this is my inheritance,
To have You live in me
As I live in You.
To seek Your heart of mercy and grace
To seek Your face as You sit
On the Throne of Your glory,
To be enraptured in Your love,
And know that for all eternity
I will live in Your presence.

In the secret place
The garden of Your pleasure
I find in You My only treasure
Intimacy
Into me - see.
I see a spark plug
Oh God set me on fire
To know You Lord
That's my only desire
The wonder of it all
To be in Your presence
How my heart longs
To be in Your presence
Take my life to be Your very own
For surely that's why I was born
And I worship You alone.

God had a plan as He mapped out the features of the
earth. They were to give us insight as to understand
what He would accomplish in our lives - and as
graphically as to give the beauty of .....
Well, I won't give it away here.
See the vision of what God has,
to remind us of our destination.

The <u>earth</u> was designed with man in mind.
The <u>rivers</u> speak of the water of life
that flows from our belly.
The <u>green pastures</u> speak of our peace and rest in God.
The <u>forests</u> speak of our humanity - maturing in our goal
to reach the image of Christ - our inheritance.
The <u>mountains and hills</u> speak of man's
rising into the heavenlies.
The <u>earth</u> itself speaks of the circle of life, that we were
formed the dirt and capable of God-given wisdom and
knowledge to produce a land of milk and honey that
invites our Maker back into His rightful place -
living in us.

*The excellence of this power
is of God, not of man.
And the glory that You have given Me,
I have given them, that they may be one
just as We are one.*

❤

All the sins of the world
were paraded there
before the Christ hanging
on the Cross. The soldiers
representing what an
oppressive government
lays on the shoulders
of a conquered people.
All the sins committed against humanity and yes, the
sins of all the people them selves. Of course there also
were the scoffers, the phony religious, betrayers; the
wicked, the strong, and the weak.
and then, the darkness of
man and devil tried to envelope
Him in their ghastly embrace
only to be overwhelmed
by love for His creation
and brought to its knees
before a sinless Lord;
its strength broken
by His Blood, its power
and force coming to a
standstill before this Man,
clothed in humility.
And even death himself
made a mockery of -
in the wake
of mercy and grace.

Amazing Love - How Can it Be
That Thou My God
Shouldst Die for Me.

No stained glass windows
No statues standing there
No priest to offer sacrifice
Only the humble heart laid bare
Of a people born to give
Their lives to a living God
That they might live.
The church is not a building
Made of stone
The church is a people
Standing alone
One by one we are gathered in
To be joined in one Spirit
So we become kin
The children of God
Sisters and brothers
A family together
To love one another.

My All, My All, That's my call
To follow Your path
Just as You ask
To be like You, That's my desire
That You would set my heart on fire
I say yes - yes to all Your will
That even my soul
Would have its fill.

His glory contained at last was shed forth
In resurrection power
No longer hidden from our eyes
His life is now ours
Covered by His presence
With peace at last
Overshadowed by His glory
Our past is past
He became our sin
The bounty was paid
We became His love
My God - what a trade!
Light for darkness, life for death
The grave holds no terror
For our last breath
Our glory contained
In resurrection power
His presence will be there
In our last hour.

Another Lamb, This One Unique
Has Shed His Blood For You
On the cross He was impaled
So we would know the truth
He bore our shame, our guilt, our sin
For our soul set free
To make a place for Him to live
Within you and me.

❤

Was there such a One to take our place
To die the death of sin
To take this evil upon himself
And be the instrument God would use
The sacrifice meant to win
The war of death and hell
That was our inheritance
Kept us bound in fleshly desire
But God was watching closely
His eyes set on fire
In the beginning He created man
To be His very own
But stolen and shipwrecked
We got lost with no hope
No meaning of life, no grace, no faith,
Oh, but God's heart burned with love
And determination was His cause
So He entered the race of man
To share His glory and grace
And He sent down His love
On the wings of a dove.

Come into My Garden
And walk with Me a while
A fire is coming
To burn in People's heart
To set them aside
To set them apart
Apart from the world
And all it has to offer
To live a life not their own
To know where they belong.

His 'Good Pleasure'
Had been trampled upon;
Made slaves of a tyrant king.
We didn't know we were so deceived
And were guilty of everything
Our eyes were blinded
To the darkness of sin
A grave was set for us wide
But another Kingdom was preparing
The Door that would let us inside
Yes, there's two kingdoms that fight for us
One of evil - one of heaven above
And grace will bring us safely aboard
To the arms of the God of Love.

The days and weeks that pass me by
Are but a flit of time
So anxious am I Lord to see
This inheritance of mine
But I am so mistaken
To see it future tense
When in reality it is here and now
That makes much more sense
Why wait for all the blessings
That God has for me
When His Word is so full of stuff
He has for me to see
Cause His love, joy, peace and grace
Are wrapped up in my faith
And You my God, will always be
So much more than enough for me.

Oh gracious God, Father of love
Sent down His Son to die
Even prepared a grave for Him
Within it He would lie
But only for a moment He
Had to battle with things unknown
Vanquished was the enemy, and now
Time to roll away the stone
Victorious was our Lord and King
The grave He didn't stay
Cause He Had promised all along
That He'd show us the Way.

The legacy we leave behind
Will have the world to know
What God accomplished in our life
And the seeds we have sown
Did we learn to love
Not just our own kind
But people from another place
And bring them to mind
They have needs same as us
But the greatest of them all
Is to know the Father
To answer His call
So we can spread the Word
To touch the deepest part
As they come to know the Lord
And give Him their heart.

Captain victorious
He stands in golden attire
With predestination
His heart on fire
Eager to gather His saints to Himself
He calls to His valiant ones
These are ready to hear His voice
These are ready to rejoice
As they join with Him in one accord
Forever with their Lord.

The God of love
So merciful and good
Though sin had borne His touch
He chose to treat us with respect
Though no one else would
He never did abandon us
Nor ever turned His back
We had to work for what we had
But never was there lack
He knew what man would do
So He made a future plan
No matter what the cost
He would get us back
So He went to the cross
He paid the price
Redemption set us free
I'm so glad His love and grace
Transferred to me.

All the world witnessed
As He hung on that cross
For a people enveloped in sin
For a people that was lost
No thought given to His own demise
The pain and suffering
As His last breath lingered
Till He accomplished one thing
To cast forth His forgiveness
And cleansing from their shame
Cause after all that's said and done
That's why He came
His love was overwhelmed
By the cause in His heart
That He would have a people set apart
That in the depths of their soul
The anguish of their sin
Would search for a freedom
To their life from within
So He sent forth His Spirit
To seek and search for them
If they would truly want
To belong to Ha Shem
So by His Spirit conquered
The evil one at last -
And Spirit life came forth,
As His love abroad was cast.

❤

All I ask of You, Lord
Is to walk in the garden
Of Your pleasure
If I am Your treasure
For all I require of You
Is that I may know You
Know an intimacy with You
That is for no one else
That I may hold Your hand
And enter in
Breath of Heaven
Hear me now
As my heart races
With the knowledge of Your love
Oh mighty Wind of God
Let Your Spirit flow through me
Let Your life awaken my soul
That I may know You.

Oh mighty wind of God
Blow Your flame of fire
On a people hungry to know You
To lift us out of this mire
Into Your heavenlies
Into Your glory and grace
Into Your heart of hearts
To see You face to face
To know where I belong
You'll never let me go
So I walk in Your love
And know where I belong

Now death where is your sting
God's resurrection brings
A hope of new beginnings
There never has to be
A fear of being lost
I sent My Son, My only Son
To conquer death, to pay the cost
So now you have to pay
For your rebellion to the word
You've gone your own way
You've abandoned the Lord
Now death you have to die
For troubling those who are mine
You're lost for eternity
And My own are now free.

To see You in Your splendor
Most glorious heavenly King
Is all that I can hope for
As my heart in wonder, sings
Your throne of glory awaits
The bride, bought by Your Blood
For You taught us how to soar
And told us we could
Now we are overcomers
The devil has no plea
Sin has no hold on us
Cause You have set us free.

His body on a tree There for you and me
To pay the price For our lost identity
We should belong to Him
That was the first plan
Created in the garden
But sin replaced it all
We had to wait for pardon
Yes He came, it was all laid down
He'd take that place for now
Once for all, He paid the price
So we could wear the crown of life.

There's the wonder of a butterfly
Two souls contained in one
Yet destined to separate
To join the beauty
Of a resurrected life.

A double portion of pleasure and grace
As we see God face to face
Oh the glory, true rapturous love
Coming down from heaven above
I love You Lord Jesus
I'll love You to the end
I'll forever be faithful
Cause You made me Your friend

Bound together by love's strong cord
Never again to be lost
Cause the Master of all eternity
Has paid the price - what the cost
He left it all He gave His crown
His place in the heavenlies
He laid it down
He became just like me
To die on a tree
He gave it all
So I could be free.

All creation worships You
All creation bows
The Lamb God, reality/truth
Has risen to His throne
To recall His people, to bring them in
His Blood shed - Him alone
No other could redeem us
He took Adam's place
For mercy, love, compassion
An abundance of His grace
To awaken a soul long dead in sin
To open a door to let us in
And bring us home.

God Wants Face to Face with Us,
An Open Heaven To Those of Whom
Will Choose to Say
What They Hear the Father Saying,
And Do What They See the Father Doing.
Jesus Did What He Saw His Father Doing
And Said What His Father Was Saying.

I am led by the Spirit of God
I walk in places unknown
Obedient to the will of God
I go where I am shown
To release His love to a hurting world
Is what He calls me to do
And I'll be faithful to only know
It's in His Name, He does it all
And He makes all things new.

Free choice, He says, it's up to me
I can say and do what I want to be
But oh, the consequences of this freedom
Can only lead me to darkness and death
Is there none that can save me
As I wander alone
Oh yes there is...the Breath of God
A lamp to my feet, a light to my path
His Glory and His Life to encompass me
His inheritance to astonish me
The joy of His presence makes me laugh
And His love covers me
At LAST.

As the earth holds its breath in awe of You
Your presence surrounds us now
How great, how great is our God
Before You we bow
Your love has captured the soul of man
We can do nothing more
But to worship the King of kings
To magnify Your name
To walk by Your Spirit
To love You in our deepest part
To join with You heart to heart
Because we have been restored.

Not enough said Adam, I want to explore
Not what I have with You Lord,
I want much more
There's other ways and things to do
On the other side of the gate
To taste and see the wrong and right
And where should I put my faith
I'll try this, and I'll try that,
And then I will decide
But OH! If I could just turn back
I know now, I gave up my life.

I am a new creation
Made by the hand of God
To rule and reign with Him
To carry His staff and rod
His eternal kingdom
Was made for you and me
To walk and talk in His garden
Like Abram and Enoch
His friend we will be
His grace and mercy
Has called us there
Oh glory, how He loves.

I'm not my own, I belong to Jesus
Endued with power in this very hour
To vanquish the enemy that taunts me
In the memories that haunt me
As I try to sleep
But remembering my soul to keep
In the heart of the Very God
Who stole me away from
The vicious thief
Who thought he could conquer -
Overcome
The One Who shed His Blood
And didn't know this Very God
Was the One Who would conquer him.

We are not of this world
We belong in heavenly places
For this is what God intended
So we could learn to walk in His graces
A school to test our trust
Will we abandon God
If things get too rough
Or will we abandon our own agenda
And lean on God
To His cause surrender.

Your love comes down
Like a fire in my soul
It draws me into Your presence
Your will be done against my will
To consume my all in all
And I surrender to Your holiness
To yield and be still
So speak to me, Father
Hold me close to Your heart
Your greatness unimagined
I want to be a part
Never would I walk alone
I need Your life and grace
To know You as You know me
Together - forever
In Your embrace.

His glory contained, at last was shed forth
In resurrection power
No longer hidden from our eyes
His life is now ours
Covered by His presence
With peace at last
Overshadowed by His glory
Our past is past
He became our sin
The bounty was paid
We became His love
My God - what a trade!
Light for darkness, life for death
The grave holds no terror
For our last breath
Our glory contained
In resurrection power
His presence will be there
In our last hour.

My life became as poetry
As I came to know His love
For the God of all eternity
Has captured my very soul
He taught me how to live
He taught me how to give
He caught me in His loving arms
And will never let me go.

Amazing grace, how can that be
To save a sin sick one such as me
You saved my soul
And gave the Spirit of life
I no longer live with the spirit of strife
You conquered my enemy
Gave me power to live
As the just will have faith
And the power to give
Overwhelming love
How can that be
That You died in my place
Ever to be free
Oh glorious One - Lover of my soul
Because You have given
I give You my all.

The days and weeks that pass me by
Are but a flit of time
So anxious am I Lord to see
This inheritance of mine
But I am so mistaken
To see it future tense
When in reality it is here and now
That makes much more sense
Why wait for all the blessings
That God has for me
When His Word is so full of stuff
He has for me to see
Cause His love, joy, peace and grace
Are wrapped up in my faith
And You my God, will always be
So much more than enough for me.

Hello again I'm here to say
I'm so glad to be alive
You've captured my soul
You've given Your all
How do I say thank You
Cause I'm so glad to be alive.

LOVE'S GREAT FLIGHT TO REALITY

The longing to love and be loved
Only God can fill that need
For one of whom has never loved
The magic - the illusion
Is constant in the heart
But soul knows truth
And right from wrong
Is inherent from youth
To grow to be masterful
Of love's life dream
Can never be as one would seem
The hunger to be loved
A desperate need indeed
Can only be fulfilled
By One Who shares the dream
The Lord of mercy, grace and love
Foresaw the wretched heart reject
To never know the love
We have the right to expect
But God is no illusion
He created us as such
Because of His great love
He died for us to touch.

In the womb of the morning
I will bow my heart to you
And prepare to walk the path
You've shown to me
As I praise Your holiness
And worship at Your feet
I release my burdens to You Lord
And in the womb of the morning
Your love and grace bestowed
I trust Your mercies follow me
And when the eventide comes
I'll lay me down to sleep
And I'll rest
In the shadow of Your wings.

After all that's said and done
There's only One
Who could pay the price
And He gave His life
That I might live
So all the glory goes to Him
My risen Savior, Lord
He gave His life, so I must give
My life, my soul
To the One Who is the Word.

❤

For God so loved the world,
that He gave His only begotten Son,
that whosoever should believe in Him,
will have eternal life.

Even in the fire
I'm alive in You.
So
Lift up Your Hands in the Sanctuary
And Praise Our Most High God

The Kingdoms of this World
Are Become
The Kingdoms of Our God
And He Shall Reign Forever

AMEN AND AMEN

OTHER BOOKS BY AUTHOR: Dory Robertson...You may
order any of these books from: doryptl7@hotmail.com

Several of these books are a witness to what God did in
my life as I was growing up in the Lord. For 45 years
God has been working diligently to set me free from a
life time of fear, rejection, and self hatred. He's still at it.
It takes a lifetime for us to get all our issues dealt with. I
give all glory and honor to the Most High God for causing
me to come into His presence; to know that I finally
have a real Father, and to know what it means to have a
relationship with a family, the family of God.
        And He Has Put a New Song in My Heart.

THESE ARE ALL $10.00, plus $4.00 postage -
The Temple of God Restored - The Ark of Our Covenant
A Word on Wisdom and Knowledge - Kingdom Keys
The Enemies of Our Land - A Manual for Warfare
The Love of Jesus - Journey into Reality
Home Away From Home - We're Just Passing Through
He Never Came Back - Recovery From Divorce
Hope and the Will of God - Our Inheritance
Songs of My Life - Poetry and Prose
                From the Heart of God.

EXCEPT FOR THESE...$12.00
+Freedom From the Spirit of Fear - The Law of Liberty
+The Seven Churches of Revelation - Jesus and His
Bride +Knowing Abba Father - Finding Our Real Father
+The Tabernacle of God - Journal of Redemption
+The Manifested Bride of Christ - Who is She?
+ Notes From a Newborn -
Memoirs of a Baby Christian Longing for Maturity.

AND THIS $5.00
#The Gift of Life - His Hand Is Reaching out to You

Made in the USA
Columbia, SC
25 January 2022